TABLE OF CONTENTS

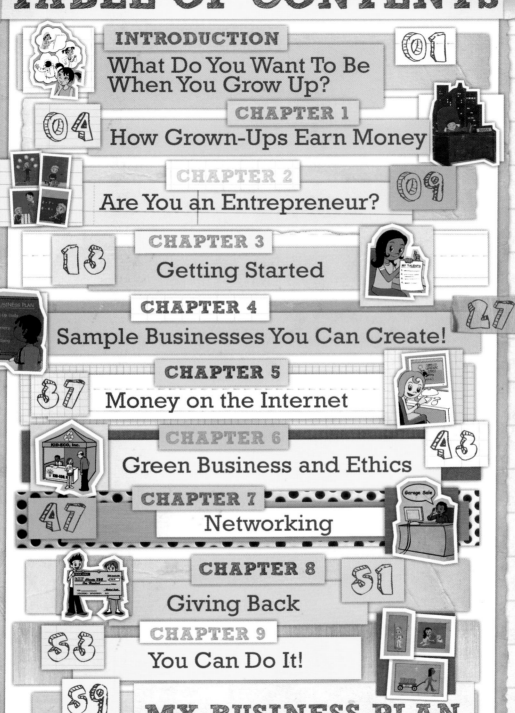

TOMORROW'S FUTURE STARTS TODAY!

—Toren Brothers

Hey there!

If you're reading this, you must be interested in doing more than just making money. In fact, maybe a parent or teacher thought you would be a great kid entrepreneur—kidpreneur—and gave you this book. Making money is just one of the things an entrepreneur can do. They can also find solutions to big problems, help the environment, inspire their communities and make people smile. We think being an entrepreneur is one of the most rewarding things you can do! Every entrepreneur likes to do things a little differently. This book will help you figure out which path is right for you.

P.S. If you have a great Kidpreneurs story you would like to share with us, please visit our website at Kidpreneurs.org and click contact us.

Thanks for reading and we wish you continued success!

ADAM TOREN
Co-Author
Kidpreneurs

MATTHEW TOREN
Co-Author
Kidpreneurs

DEDICATION

THIS BOOK IS DEDICATED TO ALL OF THE PARENTS AND GRANDPARENTS WHO TAKE THE TIME TO SHARE THEIR EXPERIENCE WITH THEIR CHILDREN AND GRANDCHILDREN.

WE WERE FORTUNATE TO HAVE SUCH A CARING RELATIONSHIP WHEN WE WERE GROWING UP.

—Matthew and Adam

INTRODUCTION

WHAT DO YOU WANT TO BE WHEN YOU GROW UP?

HOW MANY TIMES HAVE YOU BEEN ASKED THAT QUESTION

It seems like adults are always asking kids what they want to be when they get older. The reason your parents ask you this question is to help you plan for years down the road. Different jobs need different things, and your parents want to make sure you've got everything you need to succeed. If you want to be a doctor, for example, you'll need to go to a special school called medical school, but if you want to be an artist, you'll need art classes and your own set of paints. Maybe you know what you want to be, or maybe you don't—and that's okay. You've got a lot of time to think about your future. And that's really what this book is all about.

Did you know that some grown-ups end up doing something completely different from what they thought they wanted to do as kids? Sometimes it's because they changed their minds once they got older, but other times it's because they didn't have a plan to help them make their dreams come true.

That means that the best time to start planning for your future as a grown-up is right now! But to do that, you need to understand a little bit about the grown-up world.

This book will help you do that, and it will also show you an exciting way that you can make your own money, starting right now!

That's right! You don't have to wait until you're an adult to start learning about business and making a good living at it. In fact, the sooner you learn about business, the easier it will be to decide what you want to do when you grow up.

So, what is this effective way to make your own money? Become an **entrepreneur!** (ahn-truh-pruh-noor)

Now, if you don't know what an entrepreneur is, don't worry. We're going to explain all of that, and also show you why being an entrepreneur can be a lot of fun!

Ready to get started? Let's begin by learning a little about the grown-up business world.

TIPS FOR READING THIS BOOK!

This book has been written and designed for learning and fun! With that in mind, make sure you have a pen or a pencil and some paper with you at all times because we have placed fun facts, games and challenges for you along the way. So have fun, be creative and, most importantly, learn. Enjoy!

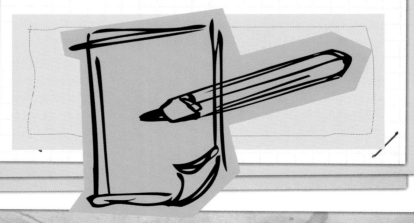

CHAPTER 1

HOW GROWN-UPS EARN MONEY

While you're at school during the day, your parents are likely doing something to make money. Maybe they work in a store, a big factory, an office downtown or an office at home. When your parents go to work, they earn money to buy food, clothes, and all those toys for you!

Even though all grown-ups have to work somewhere, they can choose what kind of work they'd like to do. For example, a person who really likes math and science might decide to become an engineer. Someone else might want to be a teacher, or a doctor, or they might decide to make money by writing books for other people to read. There are many, many ways that grown-ups can make money. All they have to do is decide what kind of job they want and go after it.

Now, in many jobs you will work for someone else. This person is called a **boss**, and the worker (the person doing the job) is called an **employee**. In this type of job, the boss tells the employees what needs to be done and shows them how to do it. Before the employees start their job, they make an agreement with the boss about how much money they will earn and how often they will be paid for doing the work. Some employees are paid once a week, some are paid once a month, and some are even paid every two weeks. It doesn't matter how much the company makes—the employees will still get the same amount of money each month. This kind of job works really well for some people and is a great way to make money!

But there is another kind of job where the employee is also the boss! This kind of worker is called an entrepreneur, and as you'll see, it can be very different from working for someone else.

WHAT IS AN ENTREPRENEUR ?

An entrepreneur is someone who owns his or her own business and works for himself or herself instead of someone else. This kind of person gets to make all the decisions a boss would normally make, plus do the work! That is not to say that they don't have employees, too, but starting out they might be responsible for most of the work themselves.

You're probably thinking that doesn't sound like much fun, so why would someone want to be an entrepreneur?

When you work for someone else, your boss decides how much money you're going to get. But when you are an entrepreneur, you can control how much money you make by how much work you want to do.

For example, a mechanic is a person who makes money by fixing cars. If the mechanic is an employee, he has to do the work that his boss gives him, and he must work when his boss wants him to. If the mechanic wants to go on vacation, he must first ask the boss for permission. But if the mechanic is an entrepreneur, he is his own boss. He gets to choose when he works and can take a vacation any time he wants to. If the mechanic wants to make extra money, all he has to do is decide to work more.

Just because you are an entrepreneur doesn't mean your work is all fun and games. When you are your own boss you still have to work hard and do a good job so that your customers will keep coming back to you. Entrepreneurs have much more freedom to work when and how they want to, but they also have more responsibilities.

WHAT DOES AN ENTREPRENEUR DO?

Anything and everything! An entrepreneur is in charge of everything that goes on in his or her business. That means deciding what to sell, how to sell it, and how much to charge.

An entrepreneur also does the actual work. That means that if letters have to be typed or boxes have to be shipped, the entrepreneur will do those things, too!

Being an entrepreneur is more than just doing work and making decisions. An entrepreneur is always looking for new ways to make money and coming up with new ideas on how to do it. He or she is always searching for new ways to help his or her community and make the world a better place. Entrepreneurs like to try new things and aren't afraid to try something they've never done before.

? DID YOU KNOW?

The word "entrepreneur" is derived from the old French word "entreprendre," which means "to undertake." *The American Heritage® Dictionary of the English Language, Fourth Edition*, defines entrepreneur as "a person who organizes, operates, and assumes the risk for a business venture."

A business can be just about anything. Some entrepreneurs make new things and sell them. Other entrepreneurs buy old things and re-sell them for more money than they paid for them. You can buy and sell things from the Internet, too! One website called eBay® is where people sell all kinds of new and used products to make money. Entrepreneurs also provide services and charge people money for doing things like lawn-mowing, house cleaning, and pet care.

And you know what? You don't have to be a grown-up to be an entrepreneur! In fact, anyone can be an entrepreneur if they really want to, no matter how old they are. All you need is an idea and the desire to make it work! Just because you're working for yourself doesn't mean you have to start or run your business alone.

The key to being an entrepreneur is to pick a product or service that you can provide and then find a way to make customers want it. This book will help you learn how to choose a business and how to find customers that want what you're selling. Before we do that, let's take a look at what it takes to become an entrepreneur and some of the things you can expect when you own your own business.

JUST FOR FUN!

Help the Kidpreneur find his way to starting his business!

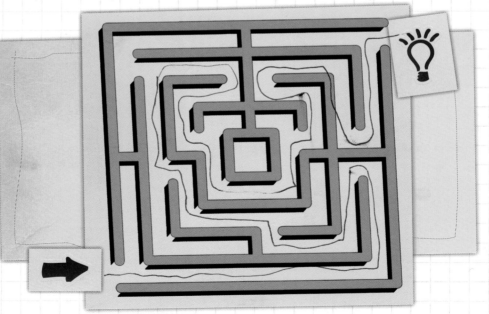

CHAPTER 1

QUIZ

 The person you work for is called a...

a. Employee   b. Boss   c. Entrepreneur

 An entrepreneur is someone who owns their own...

a. Business   b. Car   c. Pet

 What does an entrepreneur do?

a. Anything & everything   b. Nothing   c. All of the above

 A business can be just about anything.

a. True   b. False   c. I don't know

 The word "entrepreneur" is derived from...

a. a French word   b. a German word   c. a Dutch word

 ANSWERS   5 = a   4 = a   3 = a   2 = a   1 = b

!
4 to 5 correct = You're ready to read Chapter 2!
2 to 3 correct = Maybe look over Chapter 1 again?
Only 1 correct = Try again!

CHAPTER 2

ARE YOU AN ENTREPRENEUR?

As we've already seen, different people like to do different things. Some people like to make things with their hands, while others might prefer to sell things, like cars or houses.

An entrepreneur is someone who isn't afraid to try new things and who is always looking for new ideas and suggestions. An entrepreneur also likes talking to people and being creative. They excel in making challenging decisions and don't mind working hard to get what they want.

DOES THAT SOUND LIKE YOU

If you want to become an entrepreneur, you'll have to learn to listen to what other people say about your product or service. Some people will like it, but others won't, and you must learn to not get upset or discouraged when that happens. Instead, find out why the customer didn't like the product and see if there is something you can do to fix the problem.

If you have a lemonade stand and a customer tells you that your lemonade is too sour, you might want to think about adding more sugar to your next batch. To make sure your customer comes back for seconds, you might also want to offer them a free cup since the first one didn't taste as good as it should have. This is what grown-ups call customer service, and it's a good way to do business.

A good entrepreneur also knows how to sell his or her product or service. Remember that you're in business for yourself, so if you want to make money, you have to talk to people and show them why they should buy what you're selling.

As an entrepreneur, you won't get a regular amount of money every month. Your money comes from what you sell, so how much you make will depend on you. Some days you might make a lot of money, but on other days you might not make any money at all. To make sure this doesn't become a problem, you must learn to manage your money. This means that if you make $20 today, you save some of that money for the days you don't make anything at all. That way, you can still buy the lemons and sugar you need for a fresh pitcher of lemonade and stay open for business. So, what do you think? Do you have what it takes to be an entrepreneur?

Working for yourself is a great way to learn about business and money. These are tools you'll need when you get older, so if you learn them now, you'll be able to handle things in the grown-up world.

THINK YOU MIGHT BE AN ENTREPRENEUR? SEE HOW MANY OF THESE DESCRIPTIONS SOUND LIKE YOU:

YES NO MAYBE → **Creative** ←

YES NO MAYBE **Likes people**

YES NO MAYBE **Likes to talk**

YES NO MAYBE **Likes to solve problems**

YES NO MAYBE **Interested in making money**

YES NO MAYBE **Likes being in charge**

YES NO MAYBE **Has great ideas**

There are actually several ways you can become an entrepreneur—the key is to find something you're good at and something that you enjoy. So, let's start there and look at how you can choose the right business for you.

CHAPTER 2

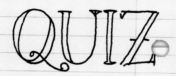

1 A good entrepreneur is someone who isn't afraid to...

(a.) Try new things   b. Walk the dog   c. Do nothing

 Becoming an entrepreneur means learning to...

a. Ignore people   (b.) Listen to people   c. Ride a bike

 You have a lemonade stand and a customer tells you that your lemonade is too sour. You might want to consider...

(a.) Not charging them   b. Charging them more   c. Ignoring them

 ANSWERS   3 = a   2 = b   1 = a

3 correct = You're ready to read Chapter 3!
2 correct = Maybe look over Chapter 2 again?
Only 1 correct = Try again!

CHAPTER 3

GETTING STARTED

Now that you've learned what an entrepreneur does, you're ready to begin your own adventure in the world of business.

The first thing you'll have to do is decide on what kind of business you want to run. Just like adults, you can choose almost any kind of business you want, as long as it's something you can safely do by yourself or with your friends, and something that your parents or guardians approve of.

CHOOSING YOUR BUSINESS

To choose the right business for you, let's start by making a list of all the things you like to do. What are your hobbies? What games do you like to play? What classes do you like in school? Do you play a musical instrument? Do you know how to use a lawn mower or ride a bike? Do you like animals?

Write down everything that you can do and then look at your list. How can you turn your skills and talents into money-making ideas?

For example, if you can ride a bike, you might want to start an errand service. In this type of business, you would offer to go get things for your customers (your neighbors), such as a gallon of milk or a loaf of bread from the store. In exchange for picking up their items, they would pay you a fee.

Can you use a lawn mower? If you can, you could start your own lawn-care business and mow your neighbors' lawns for cash. Are you good in math or reading? Offer a tutoring service. Know how to type? You could become a **virtual assistant**, which means that you offer typing and basic office services from your own home.

Still trying to figure out the right business for you? How about window washing, raking leaves, or walking your neighbors' dogs? You could

KIDPRENEURS CHALLENGE

Think of and write down the three things you're the best at!
1. Craft   2. Reading   3. Singing

sell homemade cookies, offer babysitting or pet sitting services, or shovel sidewalks in the winter. The point is, there are plenty of ways to make money and start your very first business. You just have to be creative and think like an entrepreneur.

Go over your list of talents and skills and make notes about the different jobs each one could create. And as you're thinking about your new business, here are a few other things that you need to consider:

START-UP COSTS

Starting a new business is going to take some money. How much money will depend upon the business you choose. For example, to open a lemonade stand, you'll need to buy paper cups for your customers to drink from. You'll need a table or stand of some sort to set everything out on, and you'll also need some paints or markers to make your sign. And let's not forget, you'll need to buy the ingredients to make the lemonade. A dog-walking business, on the other hand, doesn't require a lot of money to get started. You might need to purchase leashes if your customers don't have one or can't find theirs, but other than that, all you will need are your own two feet.

When choosing your business, think about what you'll have to buy in order to get started. Will your product require ingredients? Are you going to offer a service that needs supplies? Try to add up how much these things might cost and then decide if it's something you can do. There are basically two ways to get the money you'll need for your start-up costs: you can borrow from your parents, or you can use your own allowance to buy the supplies you need. If you've decided to partner with some of your friends, combining your allowances might work, but if you're doing your business by yourself, you may have to ask Mom and Dad for a little financial help.

DID YOU KNOW ?

The *New York Times* credited Henry E. Allott as the inventor of pink lemonade:

At 15 he ran away with a circus and obtained the lemonade concession. One day while mixing a tub of the orthodox yellow kind, he dropped some red cinnamon candies in by mistake. The resulting rose-tinted mixture sold so surprisingly well that he continued to dispense his chance discovery.

Another option for your start-up costs would be finding a sponsor. A sponsor is someone—usually a businessperson, teacher, parent, or other grown-up in your community—who likes your idea and wants to help you get it off the ground. Some communities offer programs to help connect sponsors with young entrepreneurs just like you! Talk to your parents to see if this might be an option for you.

ADVERTISING YOUR BUSINESS

Advertising is just a big word for telling people about your business. When you watch television and a commercial comes on for a new game or toy, that's advertising. The company selling the toy or game wants you to buy their product, so they make sure that it looks really cool by showing other kids playing with it and having fun. They show you how it flips or flies or bounces so that you'll say, "Yeah! I want that!"

To get customers to buy your product or service, you'll have to do the same thing. There are several different ways you can advertise your business. One way is to put up flyers around the neighborhood or go door to door and pass them out. You can hang a sign in front of your business or make business cards and give them to your family, friends, and neighbors.

Each of these advertising methods will cost a little bit of money, so remember this when you're thinking about the start-up costs we talked about before.

But there's one way to advertise that doesn't cost a thing, and it will bring in more customers than any other way. It's called word of mouth and it works like this: Let's say you have a dog-walking business and you walk Mr. Johnson's poodle, Buster, twice a week. If you do a good job, Mr. Johnson will tell his friends about you and talk about how re-

JUST THE FACTS !

The first toy advertised on television was Mr. Potato Head, introduced in 1952. At the time, two-thirds of American TVs were owned by families with children under the age of 12. The cute little toy grossed $4 million in his very first year.

sponsible you are and how careful you are with his pet. This will make his friends want to hire you, too, because if Mr. Johnson likes your work, you must be really good at walking dogs.

Keep in mind the advertising doesn't stop there. Do a good job with Mr. Johnson's friends, and they'll tell their friends. Pretty soon, you could have the whole neighborhood as customers, and all because you did a good job with Mr. Johnson's dog.

See how this works? The thing to remember about word of mouth advertising is that it works both ways. If you do a good job, word of mouth can get you a lot of new customers. But if you do a bad job, word of mouth can hurt your business.

How? Let's say that Mr. Johnson has to walk his dog because you didn't show up when you were supposed to. The next time he talks to his friends, he'll be sure to tell them that you forgot to stop by. This can make you and your business seem unreliable, meaning that your customers can't count on you to do what you say you'll do. This makes it very hard to get new customers.

So, the best way to get the most from word of mouth advertising is to do a great job every time! Keep your appointments and do the kind of work you'd want someone to do for you.

Now, back to those other forms of advertising. When you want to attract new customers, you need to get their attention. You can do this with colorful pictures on a sign or a catchy name for your business—for example, Jack's Walk-A-Dog or Pooches & Pets Sitting Service. These official-sounding names tell your customers that you take your business seriously and that you'll give them professional service.

If you know how to use a computer, try making a cool logo to go with your company name. A logo is a picture or design with your company's

RESEARCH TIME !

Ask your parents if you can look through some old magazines. With their help cut out some logos that you like and paste them here!

paste logo here	paste logo here	paste logo here	paste logo here	paste logo here

name on it, such as the big M on the McDonalds® sign. If you can't use a computer, don't worry—you can cut out some pictures from a magazine or even draw your own! The point is to make something that attracts attention, whether it's a big sign, some fancy business cards, or some colorful flyers. The "bigger" you think, the better your business will be!

DECIDING WHAT TO CHARGE

Another thing you'll need to decide is how much you want to charge for your product or service.

Look at those start-up costs we talked about earlier and keep them in mind when deciding how much money to charge. You don't want to sell lemonade for 25¢ per cup if it costs you more than that to make it. Get your mom and dad to help you figure out how much you'll have to spend in order to provide the product or service you're selling. This is done by dividing your start-up costs by the number of products you can make. For example, if it cost you $5.00 to buy the ingredients for lemonade and that $5.00 will make 20 cups, divide $5.00 by 20 to get 25¢—that means it's costing you 25¢ to make one cup of lemonade.

If you're only charging 25¢, then you're not really making any money. Once you've sold 20 cups of lemonade, you would have to make another pitcher and that means another $5—but there would be no money left over for you!

This is how business works, and as an entrepreneur, your job is to figure out how to provide the best service or product for the customer. You want to charge them a fair price, but you want to make sure you get a little cash, too. So, instead of charging 25¢, you could charge 30¢ or 40¢, but this will just barely cover your expenses and not leave much left over for you. A better idea would be to charge

TAKE A BREAK AND PLAY THIS GAME!

Which dollar bill is different? Circle your answer.

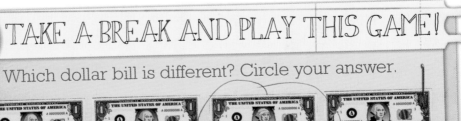

a.   b.   c.   d.

Answer: c

50¢, so that you have a small **profit** every time you sell a cup, and when you need to spend another $5 to buy more ingredients, you'll still have money left over from your sales.

See why money management is important?

Don't worry if you're not sure about figuring all this out—your parents or guardians will be able to help you figure out your costs and find the right price. Okay, so you've chosen your business, you've figured out your startup costs, and you've got your advertising in place. What's next?

It's time to find some customers!

FINDING CUSTOMERS

If there's one thing a business needs, it is customers! As you look at your list of things you might like to do for a business, you must also consider which of those things will be useful to other people.

The best place to start is in your own neighborhood. Look at family, friends, neighbors, and local businesses to see what kinds of services are needed in your community. For instance, a lawn-mowing service is a great idea, but you won't make a lot of money if you live in an apartment complex. On the other hand, a dog-walking service or an errand service might do very well in this kind of community. Look around and see who your customers are and try to figure out what they may need. Do most of your neighbors have pets? Do they seem to be busy all of the time? Do they have big lawns or lots of trees and leaves? The answers to these questions can help you decide which business will work best in your neighborhood.

 JUST THE FACTS:

Unhappy customers tell an average of ten other people about their bad experience.

Satisfied customers will tell an average of five people about their positive experience.

POTENTIAL CUSTOMERS

FAMILY

NEIGHBORS

FRIENDS

If you're still not sure which business you'd like to try, that's okay, because we've done some of the work for you. In the next chapter, we'll look at sample businesses you could start and some of the costs and requirements you'll need to consider.

CHAPTER 3

 QUIZ

 1 Advertising is a good way to get customers.

a. True   b. False   c. I don't know

 2 Figuring out the cost of your product is important.

a. True   b. False   c. I don't know

 3 Figuring out the best price for your product is...

a. Important   b. Not important   c. I don't know

4 A logo is a picture that represents your company.

a. True   b. False   c. I don't know

ANSWERS   1 = a   2 = a   3 = a   4 = a

 4 correct = You're ready to read Chapter 4!
2 or 3 correct = Maybe look over Chapter 3 again?
Only 1 correct = Try again!

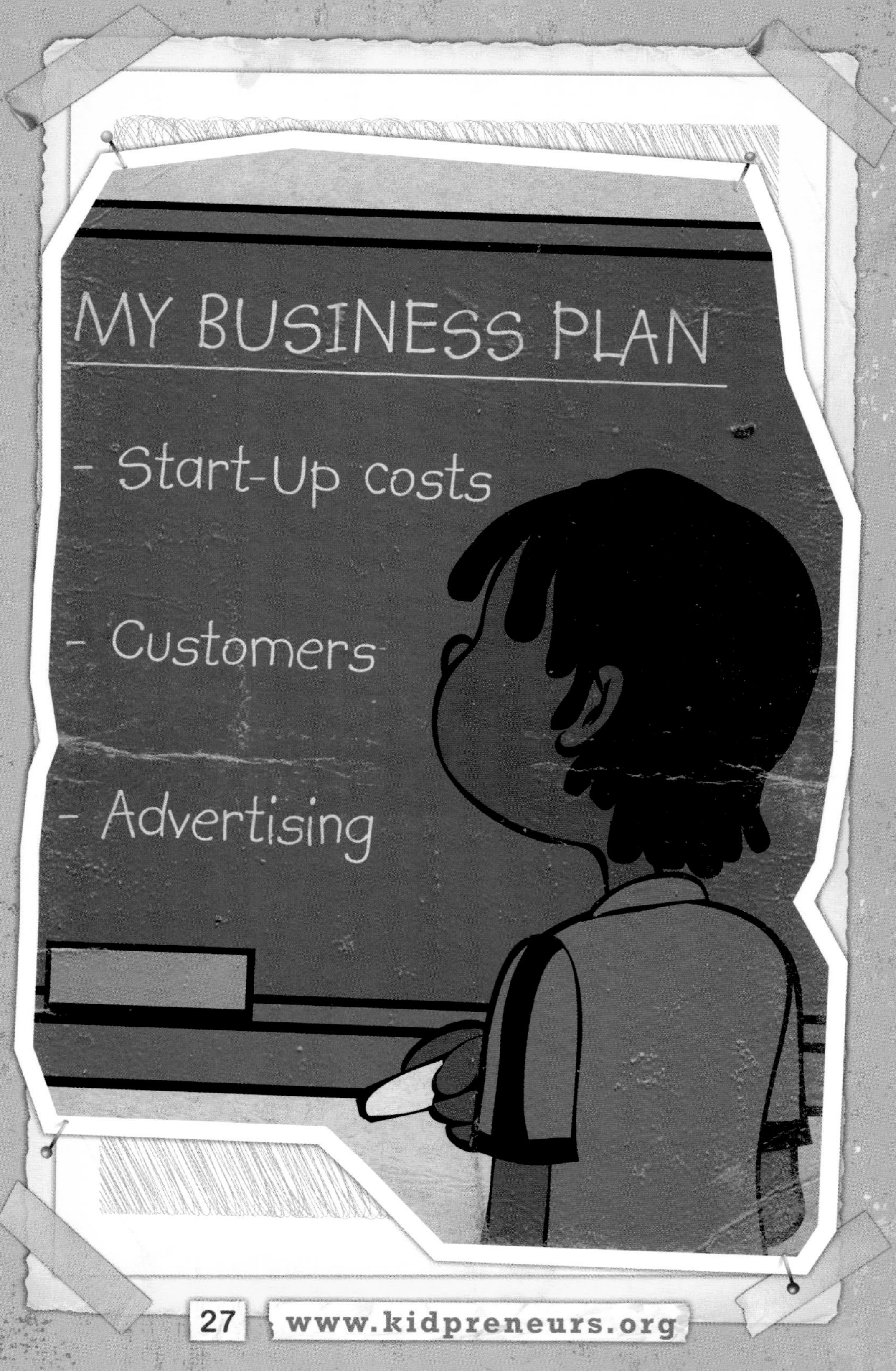
MY BUSINESS PLAN
- Start-Up costs
- Customers
- Advertising

CHAPTER 4

SAMPLE BUSINESSES YOU CAN CREATE!

So, you're ready to start your own business, right? To help you get started, we've put together some sample **business plans** for companies you can start right now! A business plan is simply a written description of your business—what it is, what it will do, and how it will make money.

No matter what kind of business you decide to start, it's a great idea to write a business plan before you get started. A good business plan will help you prepare for what's down the road. You'll know what kind of start-up costs to expect, and it will also help you figure out who your customers will be and what kind of advertising you should do. Think of your business plan as the "rules" for your company, just like the rules you make with your friends when you form a club. It can tell you everything you want to know about your company, but you can always change it as your business begins to grow.

Ready to get started? Let's take a look at some sample business plans!

YOUR IDEAS HERE !

Look at the sample business plans on the following pages and make notes here on what kind of business you might want to start:

Sarah's Babysitting Service

HAPPY KIDS BABYSITTING

WHAT WE DO

Happy Kids Babysitting Service is a great part-time child-care service for children ages 3 to 10. As the owner, I provide snacks and fun activities, such as finger painting and story time, plus games like hide-and-seek. All babysitting is done in my home, so my parents are always available in the case of an emergency.

HOURS

available to work from 4 p.m. to 8 p.m. Monday through Friday, and 6 p.m. to 10 p.m. on Saturday; no Sunday availability

CUSTOMERS

neighbors   relatives and their friends

residents in surrounding communities

START-UP COSTS

• crafts • crayons • coloring books • fun things to do with the kids
• CPR certification class

SELLING POINTS

• CPR certified • good with kids • provide fun activities to do
• babysitting done in my home • supervised by parents

ADVERTISING

flyers handed out to my neighbors who have kids and posted on bulletin board at grocery store

NEED TO DO

• take CPR class at the YMCA • purchase supplies for activities
• create flyers

PRICE

$7 per hour

David's Lawn Care Service

GREEN THUMB LAWN CARE

WHAT WE DO

Green Thumb Lawn Care offers basic lawn care, such as mowing, raking leaves and assistance with planting. I have 2 years experience mowing my lawn and provide my own equipment and tools.

HOURS

available from 7 a.m. to 10 a.m., Saturday and Sunday

CUSTOMERS

neighbors

relatives and their friends

START-UP COSTS

• lawn mower • rake • trash bags • gas for mower

SELLING POINTS

• experienced • provide own tools and equipment • no competition

ADVERTISING

flyers handed out to my neighbors and sign on Mom and Dad's car

NEED TO DO

create flyers

PRICE

$30 per yard

Calli & Callisto's Lemonade Stand

[MOST EXCELLENT LEMONADE]

WHAT WE DO

Calli & Callisto's Most Excellent Lemonade offers delicious and refreshing lemonade to the entire community. It's just 75 cents per cup, and it's always made fresh.

HOURS

open from 10 a.m. to 4 p.m. on Saturday and Sunday

CUSTOMERS

neighbors

relatives and their friends

START-UP COSTS

• lemons • sugar • large pitcher • paper cups • table • tablecloth • napkins • sign

SELLING POINTS

• delicious and inexpensive • made with fresh ingredients • only competition is two blocks over, but they serve instant lemonade

ADVERTISING

sign in front of stand

NEED TO DO

• practice making great lemonade and make sign • get permission from grocery store manager to set up in front of store

PRICE

75 cents per cup

Jack's Dog-Walking Service

[JACK'S WALK-A-DOG]

WHAT WE DO

Jack's Walk-a-Dog provides regular outings and exercise for your dogs. The company consists of three owners, and we all work to make sure your dog gets the best care. We can take your dog to the park for a fun outing or, if you're in a hurry, just a quick walk around the block.

HOURS

open from 8 a.m. to 4 p.m. on Saturday and Sunday

CUSTOMERS

neighbors

relatives and their friends

START–UP COSTS

• leash • baggies

SELLING POINTS

• good with animals • no competition

ADVERTISING

sign in front yard and business cards

NEED TO DO

map out different routes around neighborhood

PRICE

$10 per hour

Lisa's Window-Washing Service

CRYSTAL-CLEAR WINDOWS
BY LISA

WHAT WE DO

Crystal-Clear Windows offers complete window-cleaning services for homes and cars.

HOURS

open from 10 a.m. to 4 p.m. on Saturday and Sunday

CUSTOMERS

neighbors   relatives and their friends

START-UP COSTS

• window cleaner • paper towels • squeegee

SELLING POINTS

• people don't clean their windows very often because it can take so much time and they have other things to do
• this business will provide a service everyone can use

ADVERTISING

flyers and business cards

NEED TO DO

buy supplies and create flyers

PRICE

$20 per house (one-storey) and $5 per car

Michael's Errand Service

MIKE'S QUICK DELIVERY

WHAT WE DO

Mike's Quick Delivery is a neighborhood errand service. Our goal is to help you get things done. We can pick up and/or deliver grocery items, dry cleaning, mail and other small items on your to-do list.

HOURS

available from 7 a.m. to noon, Saturday and Sunday

CUSTOMERS

neighbors   relatives and their friends

START—UP COSTS

• business cards • flyers • bicycle

SELLING POINTS

door-to-door delivery, which saves customers time and money

ADVERTISING

flyers and cards handed out to my neighbors

NEED TO DO

create flyers and business cards

PRICE

$10 per errand

Christi's Virtual Assistant Service

READY TO ASSIST

WHAT WE DO

Ready to Assist is a part-time office and administrative service. I can type 30 words per minute and have experience using a computer. I can also assist with filing and basic accounting work. All work done in my home.

HOURS

available from 4 p.m. to 6 p.m., Monday through Friday, and 9 a.m. to noon on Saturday

CUSTOMERS

neighbors

relatives and their friends

START-UP COSTS

• computer • business cards and flyers

SELLING POINTS

• experienced • can help with all kinds of office and personal business work

ADVERTISING

flyers handed out to my neighbors

NEED TO DO

create flyers and cards

PRICE

$10 per hour

MONEY ON THE INTERNET

If you're old enough to get on the Internet, you can turn your computer time into a great resource for extra cash! Of course, before you do anything on the Internet, you should always talk to your parents first. They can help you choose the best online solution without risking your safety.

So, what are some of the ways to put the Internet to work for you?

ADVERTISING YOUR BUSINESS

The Internet can help you reach potential customers who may not see your flyers, and it's also a good way to allow interested customers to learn more about your business. A simple website for Mike's Quick Delivery, for example, could discuss some of the different ways your service can come in handy. "Did you forget to buy milk? We can help!" Or something like, "Too much to do and not enough time? Let Mike's Quick Delivery help you get things done!" Your website can include pictures, clip art, and other cool graphics to help people understand exactly what you do. You can ask some of your customers to write a letter describing how much they like your service and include their comments on your website. You can also list the places your delivery service covers—such as the grocery store, drug store and dry cleaners. You can also charge the businesses that you show on your website for advertising!

 JUST THE FACTS!

The first computer talked to a router on Sept. 2, 1969. But Oct. 29, 1969, was the first time a computer talked to another computer via a router over a network.

Your website can also include an order form that customers can use to request your service as well as an e-mail address so that they can contact you with questions. Again, it's very important to talk to your parents about your online business, especially when you're including your contact information. Don't include your home address or phone number, and if you give your e-mail address, use one of the Web-based free e-mails such as Hotmail, Yahoo! or Gmail for your protection.

You can promote your website by including the Web address (URL) in your flyers and business cards. If your school maintains a website or sends out a newsletter to parents, you could ask them to include your website there as well.

Remember, the Internet can be a dangerous place, so make sure your parents or guardians meet and approve of all your customers before you do a job for them.

MORE WAYS TO MAKE MONEY ONLINE

In addition to advertising your business on the Internet, you can also turn the Internet into your business!

There are a number of ways that a smart entrepreneur can make money online. Let's look at a few really easy ways here:

SELL ON EBAY®

If you've never been to eBay®, it's basically a big garage-sale kind of website. You can sell anything from your baseball card collection to your old clothes that are too small but still in good condition. But as an entrepreneur, you don't want to stop with just your stuff. Try using your allowance to buy things from the local garage sales and flea markets in your neighborhood. Small collectibles like your parents might buy are great items to sell on eBay®. All you have to do is find the items and take a picture of them, then put them up for sale! With eBay®, you can sell at a flat price, like $5, or you can put your item up for auction. When you auction an item, other people bid on it until the auction time runs out. Whoever placed the highest bid (meaning whoever offered the highest price) wins the item. To set up an eBay® business, you'll need help from your parents. You'll have to be able to ship the items that people buy (which means a trip to the post office and a mailing cost that you'll need to calculate into your price) and you'll need to be able to take pictures of the items you're selling.

This is just one of the ways you can make money on the Web. Remember, being an entrepreneur means being creative. Use your imagination to see what other ways you can come up with for making money on the Internet.

HOW TO BUILD YOUR FIRST WEBSITE

There are a lot of ways you can make money on the Internet. Sometimes you need your own website, and other times you can put your name on an existing website. Both ways will help customers find you and your business.

Building a website isn't as hard as you may think. Programs like Wix.com and Weebly.com will let you build your own website by moving around pieces of a pre-made website on the computer. When you're happy with the way your website looks and works, you give it a name so people can find it. Website names are called domain names, and they're what you type into the computer to find a website. For example, if you have a lawn care business, you can choose a name like LawnCareByBilly.com. If you have a babysitting business, you might choose CaringSitter.com. Domain names cost a bit of money, so keep them in mind when you're calculating startup costs.

If you don't want or need your own website, you can make a profile on someone else's. Websites like Fiverr.com help customers find assistants to help them in many areas, like writing, design, and even jewelry-making. When you make a profile on Fiverr, you list the skills you have that will help you do that job. Then customers contact you so the two of you can agree on a job.

Some websites are for specific jobs and businesses. On Rover.com, you can set up a profile as a pet sitter. On Etsy.com, you can set up an online shop where you sell jewelry, clothes, art, and more. It's all about finding a website that fits your business!

No matter how you decide to build your business online, make sure a parent or guardian is helping you do it in a safe way.

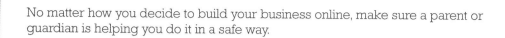

WEBSITE BUILDERS:

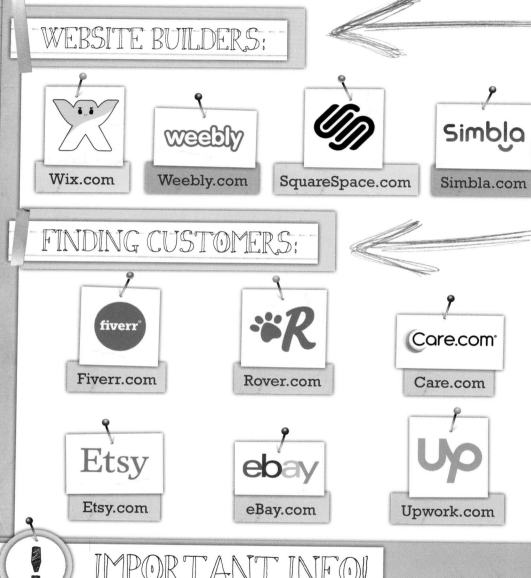

Wix.com

Weebly.com

SquareSpace.com

Simbla.com

FINDING CUSTOMERS:

Fiverr.com

Rover.com

Care.com

Etsy.com

eBay.com

Upwork.com

IMPORTANT INFO!

Different websites have different sign-up requirements, so have a parent or guardian help you through the sign-up process.

CHAPTER 5

QUIZ

 The Internet is a good place to...

a. Advertise   b. Earn money   c. All of the above

 Building your first website is...

a. Easy   b. Fun   c. All of the above

 Once you have your website you can also...

a. Sell advertising   b. Close your business   c. Quit

 The Internet can help you reach...

a. Customers   b. The moon   c. I don't know

 This chapter was extremely fun to read.

a. True   b. False   c. I don't know

ANSWERS

5 = a   4 = a   3 = a   2 = c   1 = c

4 to 5 correct = You're ready to read Chapter 6!
2 to 3 correct = Maybe look over Chapter 5 again?
Only 1 correct = Try again!

GREEN BUSINESS AND ETHICS

When you hear the word "green" you probably think of the color of leaves or grass. But **green** is also a name given to businesses that take care of the planet, help fight pollution, and make the earth a better place to live for all the animals and people that live here.

Your parents and teachers may have already told you about some of the problems happening with the earth's environment. For example, many animals are losing their homes and people are having a hard time finding clean water to drink. Some people are becoming sick because there are chemicals in the air. All over the world people are starting to realize that we need to change the way we live and work to make sure everyone stays healthy. A **green business** works to do just that!

A green business operates without harming the earth or using valuable natural resources. For example, if you sell lemonade, you can choose between serving it to your customers in styrofoam cups or paper cups. Styrofoam cups cannot be recycled, and when they are thrown away they sit in the garbage dump for thousands of years. But paper cups can be recycled! So by choosing to serve you lemonade in paper cups, you are greening your business. If you want to take it a step further, you can put a small recycling bin next to your lemonade stand so that your customers can put them in there before they walk away. That way you can be extra sure that the paper cups will be recycled instead of just thrown in the trash.

There are many, many ways to have a green business. Using recycled products, recycling your own waste, conserving your materials, and using natural products without a lot of chemicals in them are all good ways that you can make any kind of business green.

JUST THE FACTS!

Aluminum, glass, and paper are the three easiest materials to recycle.

But what if it costs more money to buy green materials for your business? For example, paper cups usually cost more money than styrofoam cups. That means if you want to have a green business, you must do one of two things:

1. Charge more for your lemonade to make up the extra cost of the cups; or

2. Make less profit from your lemonade sales

Neither of these seems like a very good option at first. If you charge more money for your lemonade, people might be less likely to buy it. And if you make less profit, you won't be able to make as much money as you want as quickly as you would like.

These are the important choices that every business—even large companies—have to make. How do you know what the right decision is? You know because of something called **ethics**.

Ethics are your ideas and feelings that help your business do more than make money. Any successful business does much more than make a profit. It can also help people and show the world what you think is really important. To run a business ethically you must be **honest** and **fair** and have **integrity**.

When you are making your business plan and making choices about your business, you want to be sure that they agree with your ethics. Your customers will respect you and will be more likely to continue using your business when they know that you are ethical and care for more than just making money for yourself.

How can you let people know that you have an ethical business? One way is to tell them on your website or flyers with descriptions like: "Caring and Responsible" or "Honesty is Our Policy!" Another thing you can do is write a **mission statement** that tells everyone what your business is all about.

A mission statement is one or two statements that describe everything important about your business, including what you do and how you do it Some examples are:

"Sarah's Babysitting is a responsible evening and weekend babysitting service for families with children ages 3–10. My goal is to give you peace of mind when you have to leave your children at home."

"Billy's Lawn Care Service works hard to keep your home looking beautiful. I provide honest, reliable, and punctual weekend lawn care that you can trust."

"Jenny's Organic Lemonade offers refreshing, ice-cold organic lemonade in recyclable cups. Quench your summer thirst while you take care of the planet!"

There are many choices for you to make as you start your first business. These decisions will be the foundation for future success, so it is important to think carefully about how you want to represent yourself in the community from the very beginning. After all, your business is a reflection of who you are.

CHAPTER 6

QUIZ

 A green business operates without harming...

a. Cars   b. The environment   c. Footballs

 If you want to be a green business you have to...

a. Conserve   b. Recycle   c. All of the above

 A mission statement descibes your business to people.

a. True   b. False   c. I don't know

ANSWERS   3 = a   2 = c   1 = b

 3 correct = You're ready to read Chapter 7!
2 correct = Maybe look over Chapter 6 again?
Only 1 correct = Try again!

CHAPTER 7
NETWORKING

A very important part of being an entrepreneur is talking with people. When you discuss your thoughts with different people, sometimes they will help you to improve upon your ideas. This is part of networking.

Also, when you are talking to some of your friends, let them know that you are starting a business. See if they might want to be a part of it. These friends would become partners in your business and you would share the money that is made. Choose a partner you trust and work well with. Sometimes having a partner makes running a business easier because if you go on vacation, your partner can make sure everything still gets done. Then, when he or she goes on vacation, you make sure everything gets done. Having partners also makes it easier to start more businesses!

Watch for opportunities to network with people. An example of networking could be the following: A poster in your neighborhood advertises a garage sale. You contact the people having the garage sale and ask them if they would mind you setting up your lemonade stand in front of their house that day. You advertise throughout the neighborhood, which also attracts business for their garage sale. Similarly, the garage sale adds to your lemonade stand business!

You can learn things from talking—and listening—to people like your parents, grandparents, teachers and friends. Their experience might help you to avoid making the same mistakes that they have made, or they may give you a great idea for your business. Building relationships now might be helpful to you when you get older. Knowing lots of people can be helpful when you want to expand your business and need more money or more customers.

Remember: Entrepreneurs never stop learning!

Connect the dots and reveal this important networking practice.

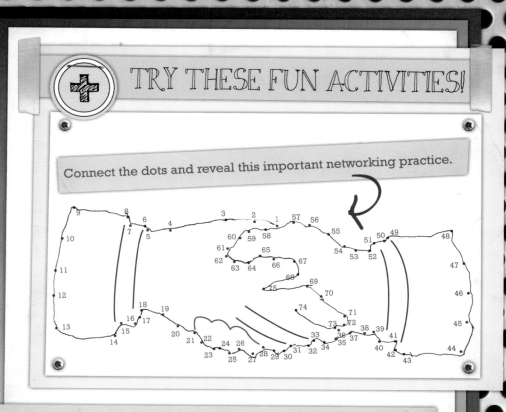

Count the number of people at this networking party!

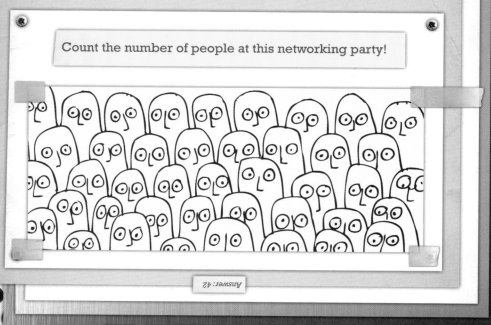

Answer: 42

CHAPTER 7

QUIZ

1 The word "networking" means...

a. Meeting people   b. Ignoring people   c. I don't know

2 When networking you should always look for...

a. Bugs   b. Cars   c. Opportunities

3 Networking is a great way to meet people.

a. I don't know   b. True   c. False

4 Entrepreneurs never stop...

a. Talking   b. Learning   c. Raising the prices of goods

ANSWERS   1 = a   2 = c   3 = b   4 = b

! 4 correct = You're ready to read Chapter 8!
2 to 3 correct = Maybe look over Chapter 7 again?
Only 1 correct = Try again!

CHAPTER 8

GIVING BACK

While you are busy working and trying to be successful with your business, don't forget to give back to your community. There are many people in the world who do not have the opportunities that you have. It is up to us to help make this a better world for everyone. Educate yourself about the many charities or causes that you can support. Don't say, "If I make enough, then I will give." Say, "I am going to give some now and then give more as I become more successful."

Making a commitment to a group, charity or cause will also motivate you to reach your goals when things are not going as well as you had expected, because you will want to succeed not only for yourself but also for those depending on you.

TRY THIS FUN ACTIVITY!

CHAPTER 9

YOU CAN DO IT!

So, what do you think? Are you ready to take on the challenge of becoming an entrepreneur?

Owning your own business can be a fun and exciting way to make money and start learning about the business world. It can also be a little overwhelming sometimes, but the key to success is knowing when to ask for help.

To make sure you get the most out of being your own boss, remember these helpful hints:

DON'T BE AFRAID TO ASK QUESTIONS.

If you don't understand what a customer is asking you to do, just say so. Never be afraid to ask questions before you start a job so that you know exactly what you're expected to do.

DON'T PROMISE MORE THAN YOU CAN DELIVER.

If you're not allowed to leave your street, don't offer a delivery business that requires you to travel several blocks. If it takes you at least 30 minutes to clean the windows in your own house, don't promise to do a customer's house in less time.

LEARN FROM YOUR MISTAKES.

One of the great things about being in business for yourself is all the things you'll learn. And no matter how hard you try, you're going to make some mistakes along the way. That's okay. The key is to learn from them. Figure out what went wrong or why something didn't work, and then use that knowledge as you move forward.

NEVER GIVE UP.

Being an entrepreneur doesn't mean you're going to succeed every time. Many businesses just don't work as planned, and entrepreneurs must rethink their ideas. This is okay, too. Don't be afraid to take things in a different direction and don't give up just because your first idea didn't work.

ASK FOR HELP.

If you're not sure how to handle something, ask for help. Just because you're in business for yourself doesn't mean you can't reach out to friends and family when you need them. You can also reach out to communities on the Web, such as Kidpreneurs.org.

DON'T GET TOO SERIOUS.

Although you should definitely take your business seriously, also remember that it's supposed to be fun. If you're feeling mad or stressed all of the time, you're not enjoying being an entrepreneur. After all, isn't that the whole point?

LEARN TO MANAGE YOUR MONEY.

The best thing you can do as an entrepreneur is to learn about good money management. It's fine to spend some of your profit on that new toy or video game, but remember that you also need to spend money to keep your business running, and to save for other business opportunities you'll want to try later.

READ AS MUCH AS YOU CAN.

The best way to get new business ideas and learn more about being an entrepreneur is to read. We've included some resources for you at the end of this book but don't stop there! Seek out new resources and learn as much as you can about marketing, sales, accounting, and good business practices.

KEEP A GOOD ATTITUDE.

While we can't always control the things that happen, we can control how we react. Try to keep a good attitude no matter what—it will help you to think things through and to figure out the best way to handle any situation.

START SMALL.

The best way to be a successful entrepreneur is to take things one step at a time. Start out small and allow your business to grow slowly, so that you have time to adjust.

BRANDING.

While you are starting out, you may not realize it but people take into account the way you speak, dress and behave. You don't need to start wearing a business suit to school, but having a clean, stylish appearance doesn't hurt! Remember to always be respectful, too.

BE PROFESSIONAL.

The most important thing in any business is to be professional. This means that you show up on time, remember appointments, and do a good job.

LEARN TO TAKE REJECTION.

Some people may really like your business, but others may not need your services at all. Don't take this personally. Part of being an entrepreneur is learning to accept rejection without letting it affect your attitude.

AND LAST BUT NOT LEAST, HAVE FUN!

Being your own boss should be an exciting adventure! Have fun with it and enjoy your success. Just don't forget to enjoy being a kid, too, by taking time out from work for family and friends.

GOOD LUCK!

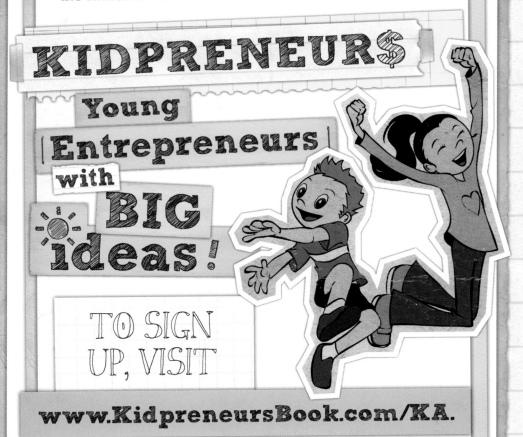

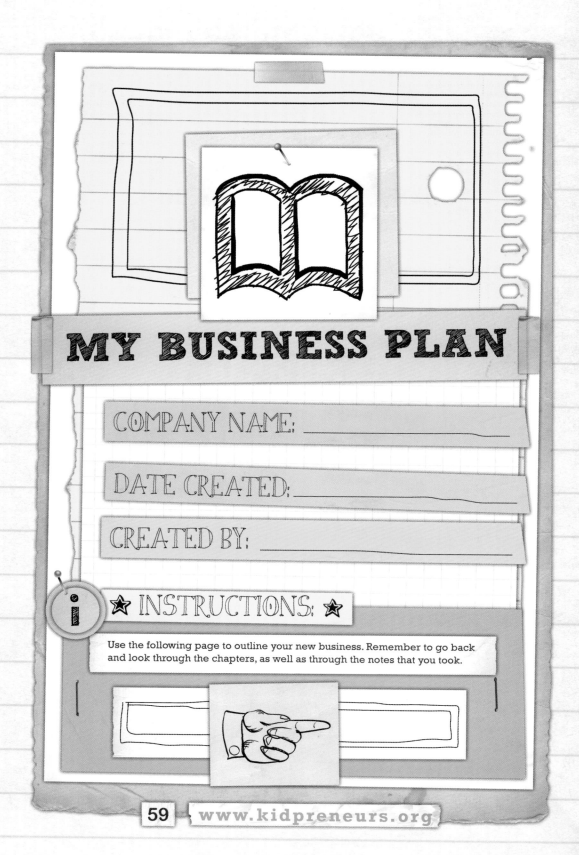

MY BUSINESS PLAN

COMPANY NAME: _____

DATE CREATED: _____

CREATED BY: _____

⭐ INSTRUCTIONS: ⭐

Use the following page to outline your new business. Remember to go back and look through the chapters, as well as through the notes that you took.

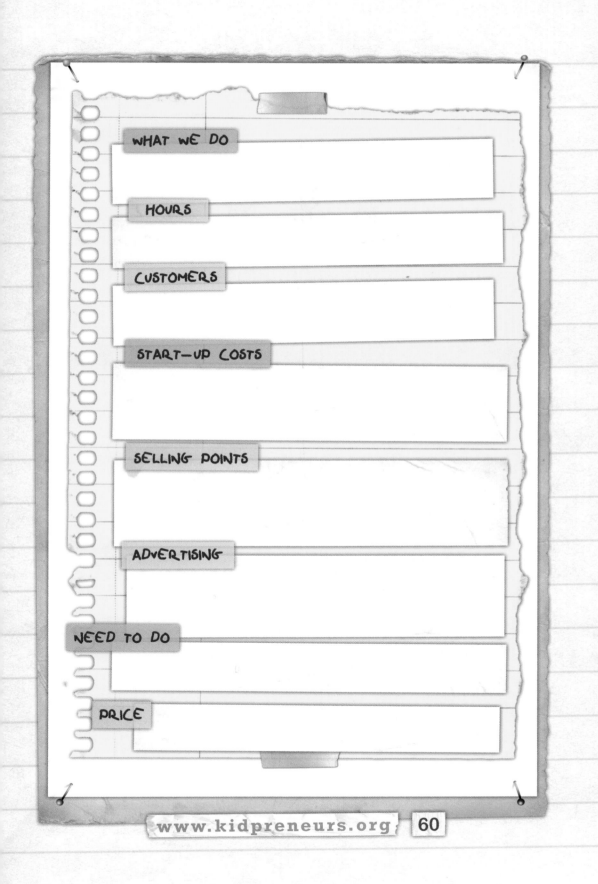

WHAT WE DO

HOURS

CUSTOMERS

START—UP COSTS

SELLING POINTS

ADVERTISING

NEED TO DO

PRICE

MY NOTES:

☆ BOOK CREDITS: ☆

This book was written by Adam Toren and Matthew Toren *(see back cover)* and illustrated by Turohny Foo. It was edited by Cassaundra Brooks. Assistant editor was Alexis Toren. Creative direction and design by Skaaren Design. Production design was done by Brendan Mahn. Secondary content was researched, written and provided by Cory Michael Skaaren and Skaaren Design.

♛ LEGAL MUMBO JUMBO

Visit us online at: www.Kidpreneurs.org